I am a Horse

for Iris Mary Rees

cladnageeragh @ eircom.net
00447990956352

'To live is so startling, it leaves little time for anything else.' Emily Dickinson

I AM A HORSE

May our paths cross again, Lovely to

Kate Newmann

meet you, for Roger and Claire Renvyle 2013/2014

ARLEN HOUSE

love Kate (+Joan and Ted and Annie)

I am a Horse

is published in 2011 by
ARLEN HOUSE
an imprint of Arlen Publications Ltd
42 Grange Abbey Road
Baldoyle
Dublin 13
Ireland
Phone/Fax: 353 86 8207617
Email: arlenhouse@gmail.com

Distributed internationally by
SYRACUSE UNIVERSITY PRESS
621 Skytop Road, Suite 110
Syracuse, NY 13244–5290
Phone: 315–443–5534/Fax: 315–443–5545
Email: supress@syr.edu

ISBN 978–1–85132–017–2, paperback

Typesetting ¦ Arlen House
Printing ¦ Brunswick Press
Cover Image ¦ Untethered, by Naina Dalal

CONTENTS

ACKNOWLEDGEMENTS

Some of the poems in this book have previously appeared in: *The Stinging Fly*; *The SHOp*; *Poetry Ireland Review 100* (edited by Paul Muldoon); *The Watchful Heart: A New Generation of Irish Poets* (edited by Joan McBreen); *The Echoing Years: An Anthology of Poetry from Canada and Ireland* (edited by John Ennis, Randall Maggs and Stephanie McKenzie); and in the pamphlet produced by the Poetry Society for the short-listed poems in the 2008 UK National Poetry Competition. Two poems – *Flight Paths* and *You Can Never Go Home* – are read online, and three poems – *Put to Loss Because of the Snow*, *At Pyotr Tchaikovsky's Grave* and *At Modigliani's Grave* are recorded, set to music, on a CD, *How Well Did You Love?*

I AM A HORSE

FLIGHT PATHS

I want to tell you about the geese
the way you told me
that someone was flying a box-kite
in the almost dark – just before
the gates closed on the park – despite
the absence of any wind.

The geese I hadn't known
were here until I glimpsed
them leaving, a vast trail of them
not yet shaped to pierce the distance,
in every wing-beat the music of remembered effort,
time weighted out in lengths of sea-mist,
acres of salt and thrust.

… *all my fish became symbols, alas*
wrote Robert Lowell – and these geese
are already moving away from my image
of the broken line
            they made
                        like the stroke of a pen
                                    running out of ink,
like a kite-tail in the dusk.

The night after your *sad request*
for me to kindly stay away, I woke unable to breathe.
Thirty-six years since I outgrew childhood asthma
(the Cezanne still-life, a navy blue cover
on the spare room bed, its mean window; kneeling
I bowed my back to haul into my lungs
the dragging air).

Watching the geese
I almost forget to breathe.
Trying to read their heft and pulse,
bodies finding a faltering pattern
in the bright ruthlessness.

Darwin believed that we are alone with our biology
but

the way you closed your eyes
and rested your cheek on my thigh –
a new unworded way of speaking;
the stilling of wings in our breathing;
both of us coming in to land
after crossing some fierce immensity of trust.

THE WILD CATTLE OF SWONA ISLAND, ORKNEY

They've lived there for years, the aurox,
since the last inhabitants left them
with the island, casting off
into the fierce conflicting tides.

Two bulls, four calves and six cows
roam the boggy fields,
hoof-prints like runes
across abandoned acres.

Once a year, a vet makes the journey.
He watches them from a distance,
the way a cow rests the bulk
of her ribcage on the soggy earth

the way the last boat,
bleached on the rucked shore,
arcs its empty ballast,
holes worn through by scratching hides.

The days fall away like rust flakes
off the useless gates. Their breath
meets the mizzled air in currents
as unreadable as the ocean's drowning pull;

wind rough-tongues their eyes and ears
like a calf being cleaned.
They are the part of us – warm-breathing –
that will always return, that never left.

THE ITALIAN CHAPEL, LAMB HOLM, ORKNEY:
THE MIRACLE OF CAMP 60
for Gerry O'Gorman

Brought here to be less than human,
Italian Prisoners of War
closing the deeps between the islands
with their own heavy defeat.

Two thousand of them.
No one to witness their labour
but the quiet cattle
and the ambivalent sea.

Longing for home,
the morning mists
silencing the men they'd been,
the flat sky waiting to see.

They made, first, a piazza on Lamb Holm
among the Nissens, paths of cement
bordered with uprooted orchids, buttercups, wild
                                                    stocks,
petals exposed to the burnt messages of salt wind

and the rough morse of Orkney rain.
Army supplies – pliers and snappers,
oiled with butter, the clean note
of a sharpened blade slicing through metal.

Grit scraped into their thoughts
but they wove their defiance into barbed wire
and cement – sculpted a perfect Saint George,
an agonised dragon.

They made a billiard table of concrete
and a theatre with curtains
the rough grey solid
of wartime blankets

where they sang in drag,
laughed themselves out of their mirthless ache
into tomorrow's brutal effort.
But long white nights

on the wet wild island,
bodies kneading themselves into furtive distraction,
pulled into each other's guilty unseen
like the drowning currents of the Firth.

Afraid to become prisoners of their soft intimate
sin, they asked for a chapel, somewhere
for the salvage of their faith – were given
two Nissen huts joined in the centre.

Chiocchetti took the pastel Madonna
– an icon from his mother
he had carried through war –
and coloured the natural arc

until she smiled into their sleep
from behind the altar, with cherubs, archangels.
The British Commander in a Jesus moment
ordered plasterboard to cover a timber frame

sent to his sister in Exeter
for gold curtains to hang
in the sanctuary doors. More than
confession, absolution, atonement,

they carved the tabernacle
from a wrecked ship. Electricians,
plumbers, artists, metal workers
became the most beautiful they'd ever been.

Stillness of their flotsam eyes
as they made candelabra of iron, of brass;
an altar, altar rail, a holy stoop
of wire and concrete.

They worked from dusk light
to dawn light and through the pale fade between –
Palumbi, Primavera, Pennisi,
St Francis of Assisi,

Buttapasta, Domenico Chiocchetti, St Catherine of
                                    Sienna,
a wrought iron screen, brickwork and stonework –
they painted in their wished-for three dimensions,
drew their destiny free-hand.

Then outside they moulded their love into broken
                                    things,
(cement, concrete, barbed wire)
Gothic pillars, an archway, a belfry,
a head of Christ, thorn-crowned, in red clay.

Sometimes Chiocchetti noticed the perspective
                                    slipping,
some well-meaning hand that couldn't keep the line.
He'd go back alone, re-do the fine shadows
without a word.

A house painter was sent
from another camp
to help finish
the dado rail.

In this new calendar of colours and jetsam dreams
the war was over.
All but Chiocchetti – who stayed
to complete the unfinished font –

returned to Italy
and missed the waves
breaking on the edge
of their corrugated-iron prayers.

VISIONS OF AMEN:
Madame Claire, first wife of the composer Messiaen,
speaks from the Psychiatric Hospital

Don't talk to me of his synaesthesia,
or tonality, or the heavens' huge
A-Major blues.

When he stepped into the snow,
a prisoner of war in Stalag VIIIA,
and heard the Aurora Borealis
it was the end of time for us.

I ceased to be.
It was the German guard who gave him manuscript paper.
It was the cellist Etienne Pasquier, who played his thoughts,
and Henri Akoka leaping from the roof of a moving train,
his clarinet under his arm.
I had no part to play
on the staves of his survival.

And once in the world –
those loud Hawaiian shirts,
the way he'd silence me, mid-sentence,
to transcribe the notes of a thrush or a blackbird.

They say I'm ill, but I knew at once.
Years ago, his wedding gift to me
– Variations on a Theme –
my quivering violin, his pulsing piano.

When he wrote the duet for that student,
his own part all breath and muscle,
I didn't need to wait for the Final Amen.

The raucous red of her lipstick
reflected in the polished upright of my sleep,
her hands fluttering over the magpie keys.

No anodyne now. All I have left –
the unbearable soprano whites of the asylum;
the gun-grey stuttering gulder of gulls;
the sky shrill with birdsong
 – bursts of familiar aria –
(the hateful, the ungrateful)
and the brown sorrowful bellow
of my unfingered violin.

PIANO MAN

In April 2005 a young man was found drenched, walking on a beach in Kent. He spent four months in a psychiatric hospital without speaking a word

It's selfish, but we didn't want him
to speak or remember his name,
the stranger found wandering
in the dark-room of the night,
dripping like a half-developed photograph
we could all frame inside our longing.

He came into the unit,
labels cut off his dress suit,
like a found manuscript come to light,
like an anonymous score.

While other patients
coloured Easter bunnies
with thick crayons,
he drew a perfect
grand piano.

He made us all make an exception.
The music room was unlocked
and he'd modulate the antiseptic
with Beethoven, Bach, Handel, Chopin, Liszt.

We were all patients
leaning our torsos close up
to the sealed window to hear,
oblivious of how we looked
from the other side of glass.

Sweat pouring down his face,
tunes ran into one another
and sometimes he seemed to
be composing on the spot
– modern, dissonant –
pieces of his own making

then they'd resolve into
Handel's Water Music,
or Moonlight Sonata,
which he hammered out,
rain falling on ocean.

It was hard to tell
if he understood us
by the scutch and slub
of our words,
or what he knew
in the elusive brown minims
of his eyes.

Hundreds of mothers wrote
to claim him as a long-lost child
as though the sea
had birthed him again, adult,
from its crazy amniotic,

washing away the truth
of their worst fear,
as piano man played on,
pressing down the soft pedal
of their sorrow.

He could have been anyone:
a radical Czech rocker,
a French street musician,

a Norwegian sailor,
a Hungarian concert pianist.

I think of him
back on his father's farm in Bavaria,
clinging to the rest
before his destiny resumed
in a minor key,
knowing that to be himself
was to be less loved.

Summer officially ended here
so it should be on its way to you
with muito amor

We return home
to the rain-smudged ink
of two soggy postcards
from Shay – both delivered
on the same day,
one from Montevideo
one from Rio de Janeiro,
the dates washed off.

Even so, I have a
thought-stopping second
when the radio announces
that Shay O'Byrne
was shot dead
in Dublin last night.

The Shay O'Byrne
who left us here
in the slow-mauving
sunsink that enters the bones
to honour the seasons of friendship
while he seeks the quinquereme
of Nineveh, expecting every
blushful day to reach itself
into his hands – has been to a carnival.

Elizabeth Bishop wrote from Rio
in 1957, of the carnival's decline.
The last one she saw
one awful night in the rain

after a film about David
and Bathsheba.

Everyone dressed as Bathsheba
or David
and all the rest
seemed to be men wearing false breasts.

You can't call it relief,
nor gladness, that
someone I never met,
half our Shay's age,
has died.

But as though under those far
generous skies, a flick of language,
a pulse of chance, a nudge of names,
has reached him, Shay says,
as if he already knows
at the time of writing,
both in Montevideo
and in Rio

Tonight I intend to drink
more wine than is necessary.

MICHELANGELO REPLIES TO HIS NEPHEW, 20 DECEMBER 1550

Lionardo, I got the marzolini,
that is to say, twelve cheeses.
They are excellent.
I shall give some to my friends
and keep the rest for the household,
but as I've written
and told you on other occasions –
do not send anything else
unless I ask for it,
particularly not things
that cost you money.

About your taking a wife
– which is necessary –
I've nothing to say to you,
except that
you shouldn't be particular
as to the dowry,
because possessions are less value than people.
All you need have an eye to is birth,
good health and above all
goodness of character.

As regards beauty,
not being, after all,
the most handsome youth in Florence
yourself, you need not bother overmuch,
provided
she's neither deformed or loathsome.

I think that is all on this point.

WHO ATE LADY FRANKLIN'S HUSBAND?

John Rae was an Orkney-born Arctic explorer, discoverer
of the last link in the North West Passage, and of the fate
of the Franklin Expedition

1.   Mrs Rae, John Rae's Mother

I never could eat the gifts he sent home –
pickled buffalo tongue,
its terrible fecund substance
protruding from the pan,
an isthmus of fleshy silence
purple and plumping into view.
His father lacked sensibility too,
was his own frozen frontier,
sending my sons away for the Hudson Bay.

From the upper windows of my widowhood
I watch the cold tides of Hoy Sound and hear
behind me buttercup fields of small birds.
Though it was to feed his tutor's pet eagle
(and at the time he was only eight)
the trigger pull, the perfect aim, the body's start,

a swerve of starlings in the heart …
All song gone briefly from about the place
and it was harder to love my son.

2.   Lady Franklin, Sir John Franklin's Wife

I didn't marry that bumbling gourmand
to have him stripped of his reputation,
built on his own best-seller. 'The man
who ate his shoes' he dubbed himself.
Though he lost eleven of his twenty men
back then in the Arctic, he was knighted for it.

I didn't lie listening to his soft-palate gutterings
(fifty-nine years old and overweight) to have Rae,
some mercantile nobody from Orkney
return from talking to a pack of Eskimo,
producing that small silver plate, engraved
SIR JOHN FRANKLIN, K.C.H
and asserting that my husband had failed
to find the Passage, had ended his days
chopped into kettle-sized chunks to sustain
his starving men. Or worse. The corpse found,
intact and fully clothed, telescope strapped blindly to
                                                 his back,
a double-barrelled gun beneath him.

I will not have it. I will have him honoured,
though in dream, he comes to me
sucking at the eye-ball of a lost comrade.

3.   Kate Rae, John Rae's Wife

I loved him for his stories: his stepping out,
watching blood seep through the snow's bandage
to find it was squashed cranberries – enough
to save his men from scurvy.

We'd lie in our feather bed, mahogany-shadowed,
watching the ceiling's lichen of mildew
and he'd explain how in a tent your snores,
your exhalations condense and drip back down on you
but he'd learned early on to build an igloo,
where the breath freezes, becomes the walls you
                                        shelter in.

He never forgot the story of his fellow Orkneyman
caught brewing a thick broth of human parts.
The man died anyway, but John always forgave,
on behalf of the slow-digested dead, such desperation.

He was an amazing lover (that too he'd learned from
                                        Inuit women).
My skin a landscape where he discovered me again
                                        and again
completely alive to him – new names for cartographies
                                        of touch.

But he never slept well in all those thirty-three years.
Behind his flickering eyelids, he dreamed us to be four
                                        men
lying under bear skins, taking turns to be in the middle
except for John, who stayed always on the outside.
When one turned, we all had to turn, and my
                                        body-heat
never enough, even as our breath lined the igloo of
                                        sleep.

UNFAIRNESSES

*Stella Cartwright, the woman who loved Orkney
author, George Mackay Brown*

She was a poet.
    Why couldn't he just say so?

She was his Muse.
    How could he portray her as a prostitute?

She was all lust and forgiveness.
    'Was it that you didn't fancy me, honey?'

She was a lover of whisky.
    How could he bring the forbidden bottle hidden
                        in his coat, that last visit?

She turned her beautiful face up to him,
    her name not on the list for his Edinburgh launch.

She was words falling into a scrawl,
    letters written across shopping lists: *Optrex, cat
                                litter, cigs.*

She was a wildly addressed envelope.

She cleaned the first layer of filth from his basement
                                flat.
    She was worth more than an acrostic.

She began selling the letters he had written to her.
    He wouldn't lend her any money.

She was the fiercesomeness of what-might-we-have-
been.
'Nothing happens to me but words', he wrote.

She was the slow figure seen through frosted glass
on a Zimmer frame in her thirties.

She had been the shared cigarette
smoked until it burned their lips,
rain battering the bus shelter
on that best day.

SUZANNE TAKES YOU DOWN

The woman
from the *Leonard Cohen* concert
didn't remember me.

I remembered the ushers
insisting she stopped standing on her chair
to scream *Leonard, I still love you!*
as 'Suzanne' draped three thousand of us
in a sway of quiet.

I was sitting beside your young friend, I prompt.
And then the stun
– unplugging memory's sound system –
Oh, yes. Suzie. She's died since.

A damp cigarette in one delicate hand.
Plastic pint glass in the other,
wine from the concert pouches like transfusion bags,
filling up with rainwater to a dialysis red.
Suzie was beautiful.

I need to tell my friend
We need to love better!
A crackling line.
We need to love each other better!
Do you remember the girl?
At the concert? She wanted to hear ...

Not – *'that's no way to say goodbye'*
Not – *'there's no cure for love'*
Not – *'a thousand kisses deep'*
or *'Alexandra Leaving'*
Not – *'the shoulder where death comes to cry on'*
or *'a dream of Hungarian lanterns'*

Leonard,
looking down on all of us
draped in the thin surgical blue
of plastic raincoats –
Look at all the blue people.
I wish I could take you on tour with me.

But we all knew we couldn't go with him.
And I only knew Suzie drenched in music and rain,
awash with song, all of us immune to ourselves.
And the request she shouted – *You know* – *the one* –
'Give me crack and anal sex …'

The song Suzie wanted was 'The Future'.

She is speaking of books.
It is absurd – my godmother
who has pancreatic cancer
has to wait for me to recover,
hung-over, on a park bench,
my guilt keeling off the edge
of Clapham Common
with Hermann Hesse. Thomas Mann.

Books she says she'll leave to me.
When she dies. In two years.
She has planned euthanasia. She says
We all do silly things. I once drank
a whole bottle of Baileys. I swore I was never
going to drink again. But even that passes.

And now I am driving away from death,
driving home the length of England and Scotland,
listening to Beethoven's *Fifth Symphony*
on what we are told – 26th March –
is the day he died. A fierce quiet in the dull sky
above the tinnitus of traffic.

At twenty-seven years, Beethoven heard the absence
of high-pitched sounds, while his ears
hummed and sang what wasn't there
all day and all night. He could only hear
the tone – not the words – of someone speaking.
Yet if anyone shouted, he found it
insupportable.

Illness driving a rough track through the rules,
the rooms of his house
like an atlas of solitude – warm baths
of Danube water, plates of half-eaten food,
an unemptied chamber-pot beneath the piano,
the piano strings frayed and broken
by his attempts to hear his own playing,
to play loud enough for his own hearing.

Reesie does not believe in a Creator.
She has outgrown the need to blame the tumour
on anything (the bottles of Advocaat she once drank,
as though
while the cells of our happiness replicate
they are all along growing
a solid silent sorrow).

After his death, they found vast wine-merchants' bills
in Beethoven's quarters. And the famous
Conversation Books, used by visitors
to conduct a dialogue. Reesie
didn't broach her plans for death.
How do we fathom the empty unimaginable –
opposite of echo, unanswering,
ourselves that high note which we
will cease to hear? Anticipated lack-of-us
more an uncontrollable ringing in the ears
all day and all night,
than the ghost of deafness.

Leaving in Reesie's flat the clumsy harmonies
we struggled to sustain; the stilted, half-filled pages
of our conversations. Sensing her plans
composing themselves in her head –
to score out time; to modulate the scales of being;
pace out the breath; resolve finally

that counterpoint of self-love and self-hate, the notes
replicating, sounding their own finality.

A last symphony she knows
she won't be the one to listen to.

McCormick's Spectacular Circus
for Gary Price

Glossy posters sellotaped
around and around the creosoted
lamp posts, already sogging
in the salt February rain.

The open pink mouth, the bared teeth
of an angered tiger
leap out among 'IRELAND'S LEGEND'
'OLDEST TRAVELLING PERFORMING FAMILY'

and, with a sleight of words
it would be churlish to unpick
'THE WORLD'S YOUNGEST HAND-TO-HAND
BALANCING AND CONTORTIONIST ...

EVER SEEN IN IRELAND AT JUST
8 AND 6 YEARS OF AGE'.
It's in the church hall, Helena
in the shop tells me. *They come*

every year. I remember
being taken. There doesn't be
much at it. Leaving the house
Joan shouts after me

Jan Morris has married her ex-wife
and in the affirming uplift
of that marvellous news
I queue and pay ten euro

to a woman in a red
satin jacket spelling
ROMANIAN STATE CIRCUS.

They are all wearing jackets
which say ROMANIAN STATE CIRCUS,
the five of them
who seem to be
McCormick's Spectacular Circus.

And I stand at the back of the Parish Hall,
its musty disapproval shrinking
in the incense of a popcorn maker
and the dim red lighting on tinsel and shine.

The lights go out, and then on immediately
and the boys, teenagers now,
who sold the popcorn
and put out the chairs

provide a drum roll
for the first act
which is themselves
in various precarious feats of balance.

It has the frisson
of lighting a match when you're not allowed,
of feeding horses sugar
when you shouldn't be in the field ...

Little children stand on chairs to see
one boy (man almost) teeter on a plank
laid across a plywood cylinder stuck with tinsel
on a small table-top.

Then on two planks, propped apart
by six glass tumblers,
then on three planks – six more glass tumblers.
A younger brother, aged three,

bangs unrhythmically
on a bongo drum and looks
confused and alarmed as his mother
asks us to applaud

his older brother Romeo,
twelfth generation Corvinho family,
who enters bent over backwards
to walk down steps on his feet and hands

his head between his thighs
– less contortion than freak show.
There are no swinging monkeys,
dancing bears, tigers jumping fire,

sad elephants, sawdust,
smell of animal dung,
but a woman from the audience
– somebody's mother –

is covered in a black sheet
and the man says he will make her
disappear. After rummaging beneath
the sheet he produces a huge bra. And

next the brothers stand, one on the other's shoulders
both balancing on the plywood cylinder
and the two planks and the tumblers
on the table

and we all hold our breath
as – no longer 6 and 8 – they wobble,
further to crash, and hold the poise
just one second less

and a tiny girl, mouth
full of popcorn, utters loudly
what we've all been thinking
 – *He's going to fall,*

knowing what it will sound like
if the boy's head
thwacks against the edge
of the wooden stage

or the tumblers go trundling
across the polished floor,
and we are elated that after all this time
the twelfth generation Corvinhos

second generation McCormicks
can still roll into town,
generator humming, can still
hold us all holding them aloft.

That, whatever about our faith in gravity,
the tight-rope acts of gender
and attraction, time's toll
on the costumes of the flesh,

we can still catch the wrists
of someone swinging from the opposite trapeze,
someone we know won't fall
because they can't let us fall.

Tom Crean, Antarctic explorer, 1877–1938, is buried in
Annascaul, County Kerry.

At the funeral, no one spoke
of how the man who survived
such longitude and latitude
could be defeated by the road
from Tralee to Cork hospital,
his stomach lurching,
his appendix burst.

And there was no talk here
of the mysterious fall
that finished him with the Royal Navy,
left his vision damaged.
Closing continents behind his unsmiling lips,
silence coming down like thick Dingle mist.

In 1901, Crean was part of Scott's expedition to the
Antarctic.

From the day he let the cattle
into the potatoes
– his father's anger like a blizzard;
him walking out into the night,
fifteen years old –
until he found himself,
feet sinking in Antarctic white
to the depth of a furrow,
pulling the sledge like a plough,
listing like a farmer.

Their dreams were ice-bound.
Crean's skin held the foot-prints
of Joyce's frost-bitten feet,
that night when each man clasped them
to their breathing hearts 'til blood flowed.

Hearing that Shackleton had got within ninety-seven miles
of the Pole, in 1910 Scott, accompanied by Crean, set out
again.

He stood by Scott for years.
Stood, as the train smoke left the platform
and they read Shackleton's name in the smudged
                                    headline.

Back to the bloody business
of killing seals, skua gulls and penguins,
guts slucking onto snow,
the Emperor Penguin heavier than a child.
Snow-blind: too much white light entering the eyes.

Sitting with Evans, sewing
through tough winter, stitching
the hours of endless dark,
knowing, when you're walking,
how sweat can form against you
an extra pelt of solid ice.

Crean stayed among the final eight
struggling to the Pole,
shared Christmas dinner of horse-meat,
onion, curry powder, caramels,
ginger, plum pudding, cocoa.

Until the day sundered into a huge crevasse
with Scott's half-muttered reason
for sending him back:
That's a bad cold you've got, Crean.

That's a bad cold you've got, Crean.

Crean, Lashley and Evans returned to base camp as Scott
and his party proceeded towards the Pole.

Against the magnetic pull of their disappointment,
Crean, his eyes on fire
 – a poultice of old tea-leaves –
tobogganed with Lashley and Evans
down two thousand feet, casting off
into a drop whiter than death
to land unharmed. Crean singing
'The Mountains of Mourne' as they pitched the tent,
the tune freezing as it left his throat.

As though he'd never stopped walking
since that day with his father and the cattle
Crean saved them all,
the last biscuit eaten with ice,
a four day walk in eighteen hours,
feet drawn on to the rough prayer of his breath.

Scott reached the Pole to discover that Amundsen had been
there before him. All five men in his party died on the return.

A winter later,
breath heavy with a daily onion
given against scurvy,
Crean found a theodolite, a snow boot
slit to fit a swollen foot,
the tent, half-buried in time and cold,
tea-leaves, tobacco, the final letters –
Scott's skin yellow and glossy
that came to Crean in sleep
again and again, like a song half-sung;
sank in him like the fated Titanic,
all aching loss and unanswered question.

In 1914 Crean accompanied Shackleton on an expedition to cross Antarctica on foot from coast to coast.

There were no bands playing,
no strains of a violin
as the ice, shrieking like a braking train,
closed in on the Endurance,
crushed it, thrust it skywards.

Sensing where the ice would shatter –
a game of chess,
of moving men and dogs,
their days like photographic plates
exposed on snow.

Their bowels seized
with nothing but Adelie penguin;
the only fresh fish
from the belly of a snow-leopard,
undigested in its gut.

Crean's spirit froze as all sixty dogs
that he had reared, who heeded
every cadence of his warm Kerry accent,
were led by him to be shot.

A hopeless launch into the boats
caulked with seals' blood.
Diarrhoea from the uncooked dogmeat.
The only light, from Crean's pipe.
Reindeer hairs in everything,
the putrid smell of reindeer sleeping-bags
beginning to rot.
It was a long helpless drift
into history, swallowed
with the last cup of tea.

The boats arrived on Elephant Island on 15 April 1916, and
Crean, Shackleton and Worsley sailed to South Georgia to
seek help.

Far from the gasp of shell, the deadened sound
of bullet stopping in flesh, the muddied muffle
of a bloody end in the trenches,
twenty-two men were left on Elephant Island
to battle their bodies' reluctance to ice,
surviving on limpets, sugar, seaweed and meths,
snow snatching its colour from their unguarded eyes.

On the day of the Easter Rising,
Crean, Shackleton, Worsley
embarked to trek the unbroken promise
of South Georgia's ice-scape.
A five minute sleep
in thirty-six hours, struggling
against the welcome blanket of absence,
the dread melt away from living.

Aware that pain has a gravity all its own,
they sat on coiled ropes and skidded
down a glacier into civilisation,
hair to their waists, clothes they had worn for a year.

Counting frost-bite from the circles on their skins,
less real than the unseen presence
who ghosted their mutual silence.

Crean returned to Britain, and eventually to Ireland.

Nothing in the frigid truth of snow
had terrified Crean like the prospect
of an exam to get promotion,
reduced at the age of forty
to the gangly child at a too-small desk
learning little, except to wish for elsewhere.

When the horses were shot,
when the dogs were shot,
when Evans was dying,
when Scott excluded him,
Crean had cried. And now,
too late for tears,

his country's surface
treacherous and sundering,
half-submerged,
all the songs half sung,
too much white light entering the eyes.

I AM A HORSE

Vaslav Nijinsky, dancer and choreographer, 1889–1950

1

There is nothing that cannot happen
to a body. Nijinsky knew
his parents' travelling ballet act,

carnivals and circuses,
the dancing bears,
the captive camels

alphabeting
their impossible knees
into thin straw,

the children trained
to turn out their feet
like ballet dancers before learning to walk.

He knew his mother's hideous leaps
– a private desperate encore –
from the table just before Bronislava was born.

He knew the cold choreography
of the River Neva – his father
flinging him in to make his limbs swim.

He knew when his brother flew
from four floors up, that
anything might catch you

or let you go. Surviving
sometimes
but never the same.

2

Demented for love
when he wasn't dancing
he translated his life
into the musculature
of overdeveloped thighs, calves, feet,
his specially empowered toes,
expanding his lungs sideways
so he could soar.

It was a language too sophisticated,
too angry for the lumpen organ of the brain.
Over and over – twenty-three times –
he told the dancers wordlessly
and still their illiterate nerve-ends
resisted like gravity. He could dance
out the parts – all forty-five roles –
the male and the female.

3

He was, he said, an ox, a dog, a horse.
He could feel the tears of cows and pigs.

4

Fearing that the solitude
of masturbation's climax
– no applause –
stole his genius, his feet
felt out the famished pavements
prowling for prostitutes,
fleeing the sensation that his body
was someone else.

5

You just stood there on stage, they said.
I was acting with my eyes.
I was acting with my eyes.

6

He read Tolstoy, he worried about jewellery,
the dangers to pearl divers and miners.
He worried about cruelty and fur coats.
He could not accompany Rubinstein
inside the bull-ring gates. *He turned ashen pale*
Rubinstein wrote – *a sign of madness.*

7

Sewing petals onto his costume,
flickering his arms instead of wearing wings.
He knew that someone had sabotaged the stage set –
the naked nail, the gaping trap door ...

8

In the Alps to recover himself,
on foolscap with crayoned lines
he wrote music with awkward shifts
and missing beats, wrote poems
with words repeated like ballet steps
sleep sleep sleep sleep sleep sleep.
He tried to say the movements
on the page – he designed a special pen –
a tangle of circles and contorted mathematics.
He bought hundreds of postcards
and art materials, worked

all night and slept all the light
away.

Wearing his daughter's crucifix, he went
preaching through the village.

He bullied her if she seemed
to move her thighs
in a sexual manner.
She was five years old.

9

A ballet
    about lunacy
AND
    about war
AND
    about
the agony
    of an artist
when composing.

He wouldn't tell the pianist
what to play.

He sat
        still
                    on stage
Sat
        still
                through the silence

                through the music

Then danced the dying
   by leaping
      and leaping
      and leaping
      and leaping

   10

Chloral hydrate.
A male nurse to guard him.
Bromide and opium.
Too much music the noise
of trains too many
strange people.
Insulin shock and barbiturates.
His wife guiding his hand
to sign autographs.
An occasional waltz
with a Swedish occupational therapist,
Nijinsky leading quite accurately.

   11

I am a horse. Whinnying.
I am a tired little horse.

MEN SHOULD DRESS MORE IN VELVET
Oscar Wilde, 1854–1900

Voices and birdsong
filtered through sash windows,
settled in the folds
of fading drapes.
After his sister died, home
was never the same.

At school he slept
with a lock of her hair.
Living above lakemist
he counted out the beat of days,
learning off by heart
the scansion of survival.

From the worn-stone echo
he wrote to thank his mother –
The pears and the grapes
were so cooling. Only
the blancmange a little sour
from the knocking about.

Sent down for half a year from Oxford
for not knowing his place,
he squinted in the blow-back
from the unused chimney,
posted smokey mythologies
to friends he had hosted
way beyond his means –
promising malt whisky and wild salmon,
urging them to join him
shooting hare and grouse
on his estate in Connemara
where he, a foreigner in his own country,
hated to be alone
with the damp-mattress stillness
and the huge rain;
the dulling fur, the haunt of hung game.

Leaving behind his favourite colour – Rose,
his saddest word – Failure,
he wrapped himself in velvet
and crossed the Atlantic
to lecture on Beauty.
His picture with lilies and sunflowers
sprouted on advertisements
for Straiton & Storm's New Cigars.

He disliked the look of Verlaine
who waited with annoyance
for his whisky glass
to fill; failed to respect
Henry James who came,
humourless, to call;
strode from Walt Whitman
who made him milk punch
to Victor Hugo, who said
How good to meet you,
then fell asleep.

Drawn to pipe smoke,
the dusty sweat of the gaming room,
he gambled all his dollars
for the thigh-close company,
that piercing gaze into his grey-blue eyes,
the gentle danger, the thrilling potential of defeat.

Back in England, he cut his hair,
married the aesthetics of family:
the Chippendale chairs, the white carpet
choking him, chiding Constance and the boys
– the boys in velvet sailor suits –
while craving an undertow
to the purity and plush,
the heady ooze of white lilies
lingering in the brittle, celibate air.

The delirium of hotel rooms –
purple tulips wilting against a yellowing wall,
smoke-stale brocades,
glass rings on a polished table
where he could write,
room to smooth the roughened edges
of unbeautiful truth against
some young affordable stranger.

Abandoning himself to the art
of belonging in the dusky stairwell
of another man's limbs;
spending half an hour a week at work,
hailing a hansom cab, his day pouring
through sallow wines, the mist of liquer glasses
late into afternoon, his genius inducing
laughter, the curtain rising
on his honeycombed and brandied thoughts.

Until the tawdry drama of the court-room scene:
the testimony of hock and seltzers, cabs
and hotel bedrooms, champagne and cold fowl.
Wit ebbing from his soliloquy
with the crudest interruption
concerning boys and kissing boys.

As dusk drank the light into its nebulous
                              understatement
no hotel would have him, out on bail.
It was a nauseating wait for trial –
the inevitable, the unthinkable verdict of gaol.

The beginning of autumn
– his favourite season of the year –
London dripping with rain,
hand-cuffed and shorn
he winced wordless as each train

pulled in to Clapham Junction.
Thirty minutes of spat derision,
waiting in convict clothes, to be taken
to Reading Gaol from Wandsworth Prison.

The first three months,
without books or mattress,
the debtors walking on white carpet
to plunder his shelves
of Hugo, Whitman, Swinburne, Verlaine
and all the gilded vellum of his dreams.

His mother, Lady Wilde,
denied her dying wish
of having Oscar by her side,
came herself to tell him
she had died. Cloaked in February chill
she did not speak and would not stay.

But what was worse – that fingertips he'd kissed
through prison bars left him
with heart-stopping night-cold
that sank into his brain,
his own words becoming a bitter accomplice,
blaming his love,
holding in place the syntax of hurt.

No happier on his release
he sobbed alone in the hotel room,
left the fine-ground coffee
cooling horrified in the gloating air.

Far from the Pimm's and lawn tennis
of his undergrad scribbles,
the page stained with summer strawberries,

he wrote of the treatment of fellow prisoners,
his name excised from Portora's list of pupils,
from bill boards and book spines.

In Europe, lost himself
in orris root, narcissus, the dust of red roses.
I live on echoes … feed on fevers.

Unable, in his brilliance, to find words
to say goodbye to himself.
Unable for the endless atonement
for what he wasn't,
who he was.

I rely on receiving from you
the 150 pounds you owe me.
His last letter from the Hotel d'Alsace.

Buried nine years in a pauper's grave
before the cut limestone of Pere Lachaise,
the scattered roses and carnations,
the puce pink lipstick kisses,
his poetry palpable, pulsing:
what purple hours one can snatch
from that grey slowly-moving thing
we call Time!

CANCEL MY SUBSCRIPTION TO THE RESURRECTION
James Douglas Morrison (1944–1971): poet, rock
musician, lead singer The Doors, buried in Pere
Lachaise Cemetery, Paris

for Kathryn and Peter Tickell

Like a damaged Hamlet
it was nothing to him
where they laid his body down;
he who had stripped naked
and played matador with the traffic,
lunging towards their braking lights –
slept where he collapsed.

His first songs – *I just took notes*
at these fantastic rock concerts in my head.
At High School in Alexandria, Washington DC,
he used to wander the wharves –
fish warehouses, boxes of huge dark and wasted
                                        echoes
stacked behind silence and savage civility.

In a bookshop in Washington, 2007,
his school friends at a launch of his biography
– *The Lizard King, His Days in Alexandria* –
they in beige and camel,
like squatters in their own unused genius
living out his worst fear, becalmed
to witness the slow dying
of their small town truths.

He was from a military family …
The town on the edge of slavery
where citizens know not to swim
in the tainted river

but watch while poor people
catch and eat the fish.

His father was an Admiral.
Some inherited lie about the ease of bodies ending.
In the frontline of a war against himself,
he hated – and loved – losing his beauty,
his liver swelling, his puffy eyes.
He said he wanted to contract syphilis.

His old mates shy away from the LSD, peyote, amyl
                                                    nitrate,
grass, cocaine, benzedrine, from the heroin.
They talk in small measures, in awe about the
                                                    whisky,
in awe – *the last concert he gave here,*
he gave the two fingers as he left,
he had had a lot to drink.

No mention of him clutching his crotch on stage,
spitting into the faces of the audience,
spitting into the face of his own passionate beliefs,
his destruction harmonising with his gift.

Everyone who knew him
felt they alone were privileged
to see the real Jim. He crossed
all the lines for them,
tearing with his teeth at the ordinary day,
smudging the thin edge
between existing and death,
blowing the fuse-box of their dreams.

In the same bookshop
'Come and meet the greyhounds',
the greyhounds who used to be killed

after two years of hardest racing.
Now they are rescued
and offered for adoption.

As the book launch ends, the greyhounds
are among us – to show people
they can live as pets. They lie warm-limbed
on rugs, knowing everything about the last dash,
the muscle-dive towards the winning post.

One greyhound, newly rescued,
patches of fur worn away,
his melty eyes seeing nothing squalid
about surviving.

In a hotel bar in Larne
I met a man who said his name was Dingle.
Jim Morrison. Genius. American poet.
He showed you something
then he took it away –
showed you something (did you get that?)
then took it away.

Dingle – from Navan – in Larne getting a boat to
                                              nowhere,
standing on red-white-and-blue kerbstones
trying to talk to strangers.
I'm a lyricist.
I've been to his grave in Paris.
Jim Morrison. Come on, group hug.

Though I was in Pere Lachaise
I did not visit his grave
 – a place of pilgrimage
worn as any holy well.

HAI ACCESO IL NOSTRO FUOCO
he has lit our fire.

Searching for a strangers hand
In a desperad land
See you soon, Nancy.

Better than his ordering three meals
because he couldn't decide,
picking through the pile of food.
Better than his wandering the streets of Paris,
his unfinished poems in a plastic shopping bag.
Better than his wanting the abortion to go ahead
no matter how late on.
Better than the *mute nostril agony*
in the sordid nightclub lavatory.
His dealers, scared and stoned,
driving him to his apartment,
flinging him into a bath
too late to bring him back to life.
Better remember him drunk and stubborn
on a film set seventeen storeys up
dancing and urinating
along an eighteen-inch ledge
without a safety net.

AT THE GRAVE OF EDITH PIAF

She must have always known
that heavy muffle – black
marble on a crowded family grave.
Her raucousness taken up randomly by rooks.

Abandoned by her mother,
all she had was the memory,
the smell of cold cream.

Growing up in the brothel
where her granny was cook,
she leaned into her as fingers
pared fat off cheap cuts,
salted the pale of flaccid chicken skin,
weary of the fleshy barter,
desolate morning cough
as the door closed behind a last client.

There were no staves to limit the falling scale:
her child dying; so many regrets
collapsing harmonies into a dischord
of pastis, cortisone, morphine, alcohol, heroin;
her voice a strident survivor
fending for itself among the body's sodden needs.

She was seventy before she was fifty,
outliving the obituaries written and ready to roll –
no song after death, no life after song.
On stage she slapped her pianist
in the face for losing her, knowing
he loved her too much to leave her
unaccompanied.

AT PYOTR TCHAIKOVSKY'S GRAVE

i

The end of Nevsky Prospect –
bronze angels keep gravid vigil
holding down the scandals,
smothering the sorrow,

keeping out of earshot
the child by the Volga
learning the pitch of loss
as his mother took his brother
and left him to be sung through
by the cold of the Urals.

The child whose pizzicato fingers
played on window glass until its shatter
shocked the house and they permitted him piano.

Reeling from the garlic kiss
of a Polish neighbour
who taught him Chopin mazurkas
in the dullness of Votkinsk afternoons

to the horrified staring
as he, at ten – old enough for school –
was prized sobbing from his mother's waist,
a bruise rising on his arm
as he ran after her carriage
yelping like a pup.

ii

Angels of denial, they modulate the quiet
and would not have us hear
the ache through his symphonies,
the frantic footfall of Ippolit,
his younger brother, running across St Petersburg,
across Pyotr's music, his breath
a staccato score, to see their mother
die of cholera – too late
for the rasping finale,
the egg-shell solitary,
the unlovely echo of dying.

iii

Angels – there to censor the echo,
footsteps on a stone stairway;
the gentile percussion of lust
and lemon tea in china cups;
the body-lurching draw
of bow against taut gut,
the *poco a poco, con moto,*
non allegro, con fuoco, vigoroso,
the leaning notes, the vibrations and the rests
until skin is silent as an empty theatre,
dust settling like stale make-up
on the splintered back-stage floor.

iv

The angels – negating a cacophony
of the unstated – the cold lick on his thighs
as he walked into the river

half-hoping for pneumonia:
a sick bed, a death bed, better than a marriage bed.
The rising water, the surging timbre of the bridges ...
Waking to taste blood from a bitten lip,
the shape of the night before
held in the Moskva's ice
like etched glass.

v

To the angels it is nothing
that he knew each crotchet, each quaver
written in the body;
knew the acoustic of terror –
the moment the orchestra finally lower their bows,
an embarrassed cough falling
into the audience silence
like keys into snow.
And with that same fear
he feared not just death's crazy impromptu
but the slur of savage rumour;
feared the glass of unboiled water
raised to his lips,
the cholera lurking the dark lanes,
the bath given, not given, for his kidneys,
the morphine, the breathlessness,
the chest pain, the fierce thirst,
the injections of musk,
the arsenic, the fumigated flat ...
his fingers agitating the sheet,
transposing the frantic music
under his dying skin.

The angels remember his first song
– *My Genius, My Angel, My Friend* –
and the last slow movement:
the open coffin to Kazan Cathedral,
his face wiped with disinfectant
between each mourner's kiss.

At Tchaikovsky's grave – the heavy dullness
of someone who has cried themselves
to sleep.

At Modigliani's Grave

i

White marble and
the promise of nothing.
A bunch of yellow daisies, dead, and rain
on the grave's terrible lid.

Nothing of the faces
that floated up through the thirst of the morning
as he sketched them
for the price of a gin,

shrapnel of light,
his head kicking against the day
as he raised the glass
and smelt a stranger's mouth

and kept sketching on the napkin,
the napkin thirsty for ink,
sketching the lip-smudged glass,
those eyes staring back into his,

cigarette paper against skin,
sketching the pull of breath
as hot smoke drew itself
blue through air …

ii

Nothing of the park bench,
its cool familiar clutch
propping him like an easel,
light fading on pigeon shit

and how Jeanne would find him, cypress trees
and sunflowers in the corners of his eyes,
would sit by him, the imprint of his collar on her cheek,
to stop the pigment of night washing him away.

iii

Or the days of solitude.
His exhibition closed 'for obscenity'
the evening it opened.
Days when he was left alone with the palette of war,

of blood and mud – just twenty-three miles away –
the bodies buckling by the River Marne.
The night he'd seen them –
a convoy of taxis from Paris to the Front,

light glinting from the drivers' peaked caps,
his back pressed against the wall
and the dreadful glimpse of a soldier, his slow-
                                                exhaling skin,
his mouth slack in a last unwitting sleep.

iv

Nothing of how he'd wake into hunger and want.
His paintings stacked still wet haunted him
until the room was a block of uncut dark
from which he had to carve himself.

v

And nothing of the savage canvas
of his TB bed, his fevered return,
Jeanne finding him suddenly Jewish,
suddenly Italian, suddenly loveless.

He left her like a defeated room
holding the wreckage of himself,
left her only the flat dreams
he'd painted in her eyes.

She hurled herself
and the perfect living sculpture
of their unfinished child
from five floors up,

left their young daughter
alone among his paintings,
and hurled herself
into the treacherous light.

vi

Rain hits off smudged and flecked white marble.
The dead less than an arm's reach apart
as it rains on the grave of Amedeo Modigliani and
                                        Jeanne Hébuterne.
Robbed of trust, say nothing

What it is to go down for love.
What it is to have only madness
and earth to catch you,
to wrap you, to sculpt you.

I JUST MOVE MY WEIGHT AROUND
Isadora Duncan: dancer and choreographer 1877–1927

for Jenny Elliott

i

There is no way to choreograph
how memory moves –
shuffling along the platform
with a torn grey-squirrel coat,
three oranges and a paid-for ticket.

The intoxication of her skin
flickering on stage like flame;
or running up and down
the banks of the Seine in darkness
the night her children drowned.

ii

Roaming the reduced-rate hotelroom-with-bath,
stumbling against bottles,
lemons, glasses; surfacing at noon
to search for 1911 Pommery Champagne
or, three months after Deirdre was born,

dancing with fever, breast milk spreading its stain on
satin.
The taut language of sinew, or the sad letter
to a lover, apologising for conceiving – *the loss
of income and all that.* His answer when the child was
born:
Call her anything you damn well please.

iii

White hair hennaed; moving open
to the high-pitched agonising harmony of time;
getting thin on tea and orange juice;
turning pale at the self-betrayal in her autobiography,
the royalties all spent.

iv

Keeping it crescendo
when the score said diminuendo;
braless to Chopin, teaching students
how to focus on dying.

v

Her last studio cold, dimly lit,
her famous blue stage curtains, walls green,
a peeling door. Desiring a pas de deux with Diaghilev,
Beckett, Virginia Woolf's brother:
I am not a woman. I am a genius.

vi

The two yards of fringed red silk appliquéd
with a great yellow bird, draped around her naked
                                        throat,
tangling in the spokes of the car wheel,
flinging her in a violent, unrehearsed tango.
Her neck. Her broken neck.

vii

A final improvisation with flame to Bach's *Air on a G*
String,
her ashes laid in the columbarium
in Pere Lachaise Cemetery beside her children:
Deirdre, niche 6793; Patrick, niche 6805.
No longer confined to the shabby waltz of the living.

HOW DO I LOVE THEE?
Elizabeth Barrett Browning, poet 1806–1861

She believed the life we live
follows us through death.
Her grave on a traffic island
in Florence – still as a poem
waiting too long to be written.

But is she back in her father's house,
carried from bed to couch,
the room sweet with camphor and sickness,
daylight held away by thick curtains
and her father's terrible love?

Back in the childhood illness
she clutched to her,
learning to trust morphine
not for pain, but to still the truth
battering against her ribcage
like a trapped bird?

Or is she lying down
in the barely furnished cool
of Casa Guidi, flushed
from a slow trattoria lunch
of thrushes and chianti,
telling the maid she need only leave out
supper of chestnuts and grapes?

Or is she leaning towards Robert
as they share half a pigeon,
its feather bone in her raised hand
as she insists he must keep writing,
must speak no more of lack of income?

Or pregnant and negating it –
unthinkable to give up on morphine;
unthinkable, her blood-line tangling
her back to black slave origins?

Or sitting in the through-draught
between open doors
watching swallows in their sonnet of flight
give way to the unmetred swoop of bats
as Robert stayed later and later
at his life-drawing class?

Is she finally supping the bowl of fowl jelly,
Robert's hands raising the spoon
and cradling her head, hot mustard on her feet?
Is she still clasping him
in that most intimate of close embraces?

NUMBER 23 TO 25 LOWER BROOK STREET, MAYFAIR,
LONDON:

for Ramon Newmann

Hard to take them seriously,
those foreign musicians
who came to live under my roof.
Lost – both of them –
in the English language,
Handel with his pidgin impatience,
Hendrix turning words into wah-wah.

I knew them at their lowest,
the doors of perception slammed
closed in their faces: Handel
absenting himself from the dinner guests,
propping his big body in my kitchen,
where no one could see him quaff vintage Burgundy
while they drank inferior port.

He was always eating in secret,
or ordering a dinner for three,
'Will you wait for the company?'
'I am the company!
I am the company!'
shaking white powder
from his wig with irritation.

And Hendrix, snorting the Messiah,
waiting for the Royal Fireworks
to explode inside his brain
or looking like a naked Zadok
ironing in the dark the frills
of a silk orange shirt,
my curtains drawn against the sun.

On a good day he'd spend hours
cleaning before the maid came in,
all the wailing anger stilled inside his guitar.
It was hard to love their gifts.
Handel composing on the spot
as some poor beggar with his mediocre libretto
had to make up lines there and then.

Hallelujah, Hallelujah. Hallelujah …
Hallelujah.
'Yes, yes. Go on, go on'.
Crowds would come just to hear him
exert himself on the organ
at the interval – his big hands
like feet, fingers like toes.

He'd have set his harpsichord alight
as an encore,
if he'd thought of it,
or played it with his tongue.
They were always stealing
music from others,
always stealing from themselves.

Hendrix would sign any piece of paper
so long as you had a pen. And Handel,
even as he went blind,
buying exotic plants for a friend,
then more exotic plants
and that huge Rembrandt
he couldn't quite see.

Oh, falsetto and fuzz tones.
They both came to a terrible end.
That last huge meal that Handel swallowed
– time isn't linear.

All those years later
Hendrix choking for him
on the unbearable feedback.

CLAUDIO

The first time I met Claudio
it was Rodin's *Kiss* – the picture
on my Royal Academy bag.
He said he was studying
how to commercialise Art
– *We have so much in Rome* –
and yet protect it.
I bought him a coffee when
he ordered a cup of hot water
and asked if he could use my tea-bag.

The second time I met Claudio
he held me close around the shoulders
so we'd both fit under
his broken umbrella. He said
he'd buy me dinner in Soho
but he wasn't hungry.
We shared vegan chocolate cake
as he sat like *Boy David* saying
he was learning English,
going to the free sample week
at one language school then
starting the free sample week
at another school. It was better
when he knew no one in London
and spoke to everyone.

I wanted to feel I'd been to Rome
so I could write about Roberto Cercelletta
arrested at fifty years old at four in the morning
trying to scoop coins from the Trevi fountain,
holding in his clutch the damp urgent
impress of other people's desires,

his arm losing all feeling
as he leaned hard against the cool stone.

Claudio says they used to paddle in the fountain
in the heat and used to swim in the Tiber.
But not now. He conjures churches
charging for prayer candles, tells of
the river splitting in two, becoming overgrown,
A wilderness place. Which is where
– after the pollution, as dead fish
floated down on top of the slow Tiber
like startled Christian symbols –
I picture the dusk hunger of the waiting poor
reaching their arms into the sullen water
careful as though to tickle trout,
and on braziers cooking the poisoned fish flesh,
it's smoky crumbling in their fingers.

The third time I met Claudio
he appeared from the crowd
outside the Velazquez exhibition.
I told him Velazquez
had taken umbrage
when the court laughed
at the foreshortened legs of his horses,
had handed the King a canvas
painted over with black –
the signature 'Velazquez
Unpainted This'.

Over a slice of take-away pizza,
Claudio did not mention
that thieves in Naples stole
five thousand flower-pots
from the city cemetery
or that pizzas in Naples

are being baked in ovens
fuelled with wood
from exhumed coffins.

You brought back fig and almond cake,
saffron and quince jelly from Barcelona.

You told me how one night
you and your lover stole white gladioli
from a field in moonlight.

You couldn't swallow the road kill
– roast owl – cooked by your sister's friend.

You would have bought me
the cloche hat in the Dutch flea market.
We had no money
but we cycled by the Zuyder Zee, saw deer
and drank Beerenberg at tables spread with carpets.

You were going to build a garden,
Elgar's Enigma Variations,
a pavilion designed after each of your friends,
all linked to the heart.

You met the poet Elizabeth Jennings
at a café table and shared her crossword.
We whooped and whooped
at the miracle of living when,
in the same place,
one year later you
met her again.

You met me, arms open, as the escalator
disappeared into Connolly Street,
saying I was your guest
in the hot air balloon.

Those arms carried Tom –
a stranger – from his wheelchair
to the toilets: a comrade
dodging the glances
as you rescued him from too much free beer.

I've since read that Elizabeth Jennings
lived in that café – every day
from breakfast to dinner time,
the cup kept filled, the flat surface
away from the taut drumming metre of being alone.

You said, when you woke in the morning
the gladioli were half brown, frost-withered
though acres and acres of them
bloomed for you that white night.

And you want me
to stop straining to find
a synonym for time pooled together,
for custodians of each other's truth,
a clue that has too many letters for love
and not enough for friendship.

You're prepared to look on us, you say,
as a blank canvas,
like the new land reclaimed from the ocean bed
– no mythologies, no warmth –

as though those deer
never startled their quiet browns
among the shushing grass

as though from that balloon
the horses weren't walking in step
with their exquisite shadows.

LOST OF LOVE

for my godmother, who suffered from dyslexia

Not, then, the pristine flat
in Switzerland. The cold
whites of the stranger's eyes
as he hands her the lethal
dose, 'administers' death –
the neighbours complaining
about dead bodies in the lift.

Not even the van driven out into the forest,
the warehouse where, at least,
she said, there was lots of parking.
And *How could you?*
my mother exclaimed,
among the trees, all your senses coming alive?
A spider's web glimpsed
trembling with time
and the slow must smell.

If I die in the UK …
then she wanted to give her cadaver
and all the smudgy decypherables
of PET scans and X-rays
to the students of St Thomas' Hospital.
They have difficulty getting corpses.
I don't mind them practising cutting me up.

Like Haydn's head,
dissected by the King soon after his death
to try and excavate the music.
As though she wanted them to find
the day she drank whisky
at a work party, then red wine,

then fell off her bike
buckling the frame,
cycled, lunatic, across London,
snaking around roundabouts
with the genius of inebriation,
handle-bars parallel to the front wheel.

Then fell into that drunken sleep
where she lost a whole night
and a whole day, woke one-dawn-on
and rode back, buckled,
to the Serpentine
to swim in the thrilling river
that had stayed out all night.

I WANTED MUCH MORE
FOR THE LAST DAY WITH YOU
BUT THE IBIS HOTEL
WAS THE BEST I COULD DO

It wasn't just that he was late
and the new hotel room
smelt of chemicals and glue,
the view level with the grimy windows
above Cosgrove's pub.
The twenty-four hour menu
and the all-night bar,
the neon price-sign flashing a desperate red
across to the taxi-rank and the multi-storey.

The heating blasted from a convector
but cold air seemed to billow
from under the bed.
A vacuum cleaner,
rammed noisily against the door
from the hall, froze us
for a moment with its frantic morse.

While I waited, I'd been reading
Mark Doty's *Dog Years*,
a reminder we'd been lucky
to have each other's flesh and love
even in snatches, to keep us burning.
I tell him about the dog,
each time the ashes of Mark's lover, Wally,
are thrown into the waves –
leaping in to retrieve them,
again and again unstoppable,
its skin shivering grainy and blue
beneath drenched fur.

It isn't only about fearing to let go,
but the terror of seeing it all
wash up in a faint line of scum
on a cold indifferent wave
breaking inside of you.

Kate Newmann was born in County Down, attended Friends' School, Lisburn and is a graduate of King's College, Cambridge, where she studied after spending a year in Crete learning the language and working in the Ethnological Museum. She was junior fellow and editor at the Institute of Irish Studies, Queen's University, Belfast, and compiled *The Dictionary of Ulster Biography* (Queen's University Belfast, 1993). She has facilitated creative writing throughout Ireland in schools and with adults and has had residencies with the Down Lisburn Health Trust; with Donegal County Council for the Flight of the Earls commemoration; with the Smithsonian Institute in Washington DC and, on behalf of the Arts Council, in Ballycastle, Mayogall, Lisburn and in Carrickfergus for the Louis MacNeice Centenary Celebrations.

She has collaborated with composers, artists, dancers and musicians, and was Director of Belmullet Literary Festival in County Mayo. In 2008 she was short-listed for the UK National Poetry Competition, and has won the Allingham Poetry Prize, the James Prize, the Swansea Roundyhouse Poetry Competition and the Listowel Poetry Prize. As well as her poetry collections, *The Blind Woman in the Blue House* (Summer Palace Press, 2001) and *Belongings*, with Joan Newmann (Arlen House, 2007), she has produced a CD of poems set to music by contemporary composers and thirteen books for community arts projects. She lives in County Donegal and is co-director of Summer Palace Press.